ALL WE ARE GIVEN WE CANNOT HOLD

POEMS

Robert Fanning

2580 Craig Rd.
Ann Arbor, MI 48103
www.dzancbooks.org

First Edition: December 2025
Cover photograph by Rebecca Zeiss
Cover design by Steven Seighman
Interior design by Michelle Dotter

ISBN: 9781938603501

Printed in the United States of America

10 9 8 7 6 5 4 3 2 1

CONTENTS

III.

IV.

V.

VI.

—For Denise, Gabriel and Magdalena

—In memory of Mary Kay Fanning

—In memory of Dan Wickett

The children are playing at the end of the day
Strangers are singing on our lawn

It's got to be more than flesh and bone
All that you've loved is all you own

—Tom Waits, "Take It with Me"

INARTICULATA

—Wilderness State Park, Michigan

Squinting southward down the shore a blink ago,
I watched my toddler wobble at the brink
of a foot-deep hole in cratered sand, bright blue

shovel in his tiny hands. An hour of castles and moats
and now he's waist high, pensive, eyeing the passing
boats, his baby sister in tow. I blink again, look west

and shield my eyes; my grown son's one hundred
pages deep in an old novel. My daughter, tall
as my wife, sings as she cartwheels up the beach.

At our feet the shadows lengthen imperceptibly.
Now it's autumn; we're combing stones along
the coast at Headlands Dark Sky Park, sifting

for 400-million-year-old fossils, etchings
left by glaciers in retreat. We bend low as we look—
as if to hear the ages speak—and they do.

Here's a relic of a mollusk valve, crenelated inarticulata,
little wing of something long flown. Here's one:
like a Zen eye looking up, an open ensō pressed

onto a pebble. Look at this one: shadow of a curved
spine, floating for eons on a stone, a tiny cuticle
of bone, ancient ultrasound of someone

no one's ever known. They're gone when I turn to look,
my family shrinking far down shore as they bend
to shells and stones. Behind me already, a sundown

wind shivers the pines. I don't need to look to see
the gone world here. The season of erasure nears.
Soon the shore will be a slash of white, the lake

a swath of black inseparable from sky. Even now
the wind bears news of another world breaking
into being beyond—of winter's towering, gale-thrown

waves, shouldering massive sheets of jagged crystal,
a stacked and aching wall of shattered cathedrals along
the beach. May this then be prayer before the muted hour

of ruin and ice, before the rise of the desolate era.
May this be stone in your hand. May this speak
of the depths of love, of how I held them all

as close as I could and for as long, of how we played
and breathed in every summer's golden, going light.
Of how we stood together here, where once there was a sea.

I.

DEADHEADING

Leaning across the bed, you squint
into shadows, pinch a ragged bloom,

show me where to snip above the joint.
You need to cut the death away

to make space, you say, tossing a bouquet
of spent stems on a pile. Shears in hand,

you eye the asters, zinnias, feverfew. I follow,
not always knowing if you're talking to me

or the flowers. This is the summer we've
transformed our yard into a spilled rainbow

of gardens. This is the summer our niece,
only days from now, will die by suicide,

followed by my mother in hospice.
But this morning you walk before me

in dappled sun, lean into a splayed corona
of wildflowers, snipping, pulling away.

Holding a lopped white flag of daisies
and yanked weeds, death heaped and strewn

around us in mounds, you turn to find me lost
in some thicket of memory or worry, eyeing

some darkness in me, in us. *Now the energy*
can shift toward growth, with room for new life

to get through. You plunge your hand into
my chest, clutching at a tough vine, choked

and overgrown. *Your turn*, you say. No—
you're only handing me the shears.

THE THORN BIRDS

—for my mother

Through nettles of casual chatter
the question flutters in again.
For the fourth time this week, you ask
what it was—the title of that novel
you've read so many times. The one
you loved so much you once framed
its cover and hung it on your wall.

This morning, I open a window
of time, hoping it will help.
Let's give it a minute, I say,
let's see if it comes to you.
You glance up, fingertip to your lips,
the way I imagine you might have
as a girl, given a problem to solve.

Everything goes, you'd said only yesterday—
of the teeth, the ears, the eyes—before
the white-coated ophthalmologist
swooped in to stick a needle
into both of your irises.

Now you squint into the ink-black vines
of yet another thickening dark,
toward the sting of what escapes you.
The way you've pressed your heart,
your whole life, toward the face of God
and love, readying to sing its missing name.

SNOW AND ROSES

—Gerald A. Fanning, May 19, 1929-April 22, 2013

Make it quick, my brother said,
pressing his phone to your cold ear,
a priest waiting beyond the hospital curtain
to administer last rites. *Dad, I'm not sure*
if you can hear me, I stammered from
a hundred miles away. *I love you.*
After hanging up, I walked out of my office
into the light of early spring, crossed
the parking lot, opened the heavy door
of the church I never visit. I still love
empty sanctuaries, the day's chatter
and engines hushed, votives flickering,
the floor rainbow-stained, the air
a hint of incense and lingering prayer.
Kneeling in the first pew, I stared up
at a wooden Christ, at some gilded Latin
phrase over the crucifix that meant
nothing to me, one you likely knew well.
Father—may I call you that, now that
you're gone? Here we are, still, on opposite
shores, a new sea of indecipherable
silence between us. Listen, father statue,
father stone, the test is over, and we
failed. But maybe grief will teach me
to translate your mute dialect into love.
Help me trace the letters, now. Sound out
your words in my tongue. I need to learn
what this means. I need to know this by heart.

MODEL NATION

—for Gabriel, age sixteen

As you speak, new worlds rise in your eyes.
A voice within your voice—do you hear it, too?—
could fill a whole sea with whale song. It sings
fathom and *league*, sings *launch* and *conquer*.
It is ocean wide now, this good force of your going.
Yet still, my heart fumbles to fasten some small rope
around the dock—and so love is—wishes for a way
to keep us here. Too late. That little boat you were,
giggling in the tub as I blew bubbles, is oceans away.
Sailboat, tugboat, yacht, steamer, freighter—I've been
watching from the dock and hear already the growing
ache and groan of giant chains clanking an iron hull,
the long horn of adulthood calling you with its
sweeping wall of mist and fog. When you look back
and see me wave, may I be the ocean's shoulders
ever rolling beneath you. Please—know me not
as a country fading from view, but as one who carried
with love the great world you now carry in you.

PLAYER IN THE AFTERGLOW

—for Magdalena, age eleven, after a performance

Finale and curtain, the ensemble bows, the stars buoyed
by wild applause. Then the fade, the encroaching crush
of quiet. Houselights on, and now we see again

the ordinary dust, the upstage X of masking tape
marked for props and set. Somewhere over us,
a rainbow of filtered spotlight bulbs clicks and cools.

Bouquets and waves, a few more players' last embraces.
And in an hour, the set struck, the curtain-swept
dream is done.

On the way home, dear star,
the side of your forehead pressed against the cold,
rain-streaked window, you watch through fog and exhaust

the faces of passing drivers, a woman waiting for a bus
inside a yellow cone of streetlight. Slumped in the former
costume of your life, suddenly all the falling world

is mere, is offstage, a shock of shadow and wings.
A permanent rehearsal. Called back to the ripped
and ragged, script-less hours, I have no cue

to make you speak. So, I'll be silent, a role I play well,
until your eyes adjust, and you fill with the warm subtle
light again, the music inside you, the glowing real.

MONARCH

This is growth, the darker blood.
Blood of a million surging rivers, of ache
        and tremor, blood of centuries

of cavern and storm. It spills in
with estrangement—the child you were
        seeming to recede, to slip into a narrow

passage. Comes with sudden rush of deep space,
of being lost between worlds, your skin
        no longer your own, the orbit of once-close

friends growing distant. As if you have fallen from
your own hands, a seed dropped into night-black soil.
        Blood of tremble, of dying for love,

enough to make you want to cut yourself
loose from this new flesh. But stay with me—
        this is the hour of forgetting, the birthing dark.

How else will the soul make room in you?
Think of this—how each late spring, your mother
        transforms our house into a monarch nursery,

how she carries their eggs inside on milkweed leaves
and in weeks, they're wriggling larvae. Then, days
        later, veiled in jade cloaks with gold buttons.

As we sleep—stay with me—these sheathes grow
milky and clear, nourished by the darker blood.
        It's terrifying, at first, waking to black wings

cramped in shells translucent as winter glass, trapped
in their see-through, secret worlds. I must tell you
        there are days I can't bear the weight

of my own life. Days I've tasted death so close, like rust
in my mouth, a stranger folded in an old black shawl
        of selves. But stay with me; now I know

this blind crush, this wanting *not* to fly is the soul
urged forward. The hurt of emergence. We mustn't
        see such beauty being born within us.

But I see it in you. And you know what happens next,
after this long night: first, proboscis, thin as an eyelash,
        then spindle of antennae, black thread of a leg,

then—somehow—the bright impossible cascade spreads
wide, mapped to journey home. Blood of the long sky
        spilling in. Blood of the great wings grown.

DRIVER'S EDUCATION

Before leaving the hospital with you
for the first time, wrestling with the new
car seat, I pinched your tummy in the seatbelt.
Your scream a raging siren, your dimpled fingers
shaking as my hand trembled, struggling to unclasp

the plastic buckles. You looked at me, stunned:
wounded by what was meant to keep you safe.
First time I'd felt it, what my mother spoke of,
that instant mutual blur—spiritual, umbilical—
your cry leaving my mouth. Then, I knew.

Your atlas of veins, the network already
crisscrossing the nation of your body, maps
its way to me. Somewhere inside me, that first
red wail of hurt still stings. A clutched fist
of twined nerves. Today I watch you

in the driver's seat listening to the instructor,
checking mirrors, positioning your hands.
Not, in this moment, because you'll forget to brake.
Not that all the other cars are like missiles aimed
at you. Not that you'll miss a sign or speed

through an intersection. What sparks that
deep red song again in me is how, after inserting
your seatbelt, millions of miles of new road
untwining before you, you turned, lifting your hand
from the wheel's invisible hours, waving goodbye.

ON CRATER TRAIL

—Craters of the Moon National Monument, Idaho

The first steep ascent we reach the rim, a vista
of black lava rock on one side of us, a plunging,

dormant crater on the other. *It sounds like glass*,
you say, nudging a porous cinder nugget

with your foot. Like two lone astronauts,
we stand in deep silence, staring off

into miles and millennia of a broken, breakable
earth. We hike over ridges, into craters, leap

small ravines of fractured magma, the silty
crunch of red gray dirt under our soles. I enter

an ancient cavemouth, look inside. Somewhere
in there, millions of bats hang—secrets

the dusk will open. As we walk, I fly back
through my life, sharing stories, stopping

when I worry I'm boring you. *No, keep going,*
you say, gently, *I'm really interested.*

How does anything grow here? In what appears
like desolation, life thrives; everywhere tufts of spiky

pale thistle, aster, and sagebrush dot charred hills.
Beneath us, dusty sandstone shifts from ash to rust.

Only yesterday I told you *On journeys like this*
we leave old selves behind. Yet, on ground scorched

into rock and ruin, it's tempting to see annihilation
as event, the making made, the being fixed,

the eruption history, the flow forever petrified.
At the end of the trail, we sit, and you ask

Now can I share part of my life story with you?
A heart far wider than mine opens:

rift of blinding beauty, river of fire and blood,
of what was solid: fluid again.

And I become no longer your father,
and you no longer my son.

FAMILY DAY

—Kelsey Museum of Archaeology, Ann Arbor, Michigan

Moving from era to era, we navigate cramped spaces
between flocks of fussy toddlers, parents pushing
strollers. Hoping only to duck into the museum
for an hour on a college visit, we end up here
on Family Day. One dad stares into the crumbled eyes
of an emperor, half his face worn off. Upstairs, story hour,
they've closed the book on Egypt, all the kids antsy
and chanting: *more bones! We want to see more bones!*
A lime green sippy cup tumbles across the waxed floor.
Late day sun casts shadows on Roman tablets, red walls
of reconstructed frescoes. A lifetime ago I was a kid,
bored out of my skull in a museum like this one,
my dad reading to me from a plaque about some god
or other. And what seems only minutes ago, you toddled
beside me, awed by the cracked pottery, gleaming
emeralds, bones people dug from some great sandbox
somewhere. Soon, you'll be majoring in anthropology.
Across the room, you marvel at fragments of a chariot
wheel, an Etruscan spoon, clay baby rattles, a tiny urn.
Seeing you framed between two marble torsos, I lift
my phone to catch you, to make this moment yet another
treasure behind glass. Lately, I swear I can taste it—
mouthfuls of sand—this storm of time. I gasp at all of it
in passing. And now, someone else's child looks up
at me asking, *How did they stuff all that death in there?*
She's pointing at an infant mummy, waiting for my answer.

BLUE ICE

—Straits of Mackinac, Michigan, February

In another season, we won't be standing where we are,
twenty yards offshore, the late sun's bronze poured
across acres of frozen transience, the lake
a glacial field, a stacked crash of glassy shards

under the bridge. Drifting toward magnificence,
we've day-tripped a hundred miles north to see
the blue ice. Already, it's snapshots: Gabriel's
soft-shoe routine on a stage of green-black ice,

Magdalena lying down to peer into the turquoise
marble beneath her, pointing at a dangling necklace
of trapped bubbles. And you—caught by my shutter
click—smiling skyward, your arms spread wide

in perpetual embrace. Seeing this picture, I knew
I'd snapped all I love about you. The moment's fixed:
laughing dancer mid-twirl, immersed in the bliss
you are, a snow angel splayed against an evening's

burnished sky. So much of the beauty I've seen
you've pointed me to see. Why then do I stare off
toward erasure, the way blinding snow blurs
the edges, slowing every passage. I can't stop

what's coming. Days will lengthen, birds return,
somewhere far beneath us currents shift and rush.

Nothing this astonishing ever holds. *Peninsula*,
origin: *almost an island.* All we cherish is almost.

Somehow, I've walked far from all of you again,
grown small on the horizon. And now something
shattered and unbearable stands between us.
In this life I could never have loved you enough.

BODY OF WORK

Because we want it brighter. Because we want our own beauty bared
before us. Because we've lived long enough with the room's
deep forest print, we take to the wall. Faces masked,

we begin the task of peeling off the torn, dog-eared green, opening
the story of our house. Years bleed up from beneath the heat
of steam: solids, stripes, prints and florals unfurling

as we score and scrape—decades of blues and deep reds, of pastels
and pale yellows, a spectrum of dust-wet flesh sloughed
off, pages falling in strips and flakes at our feet.

It's more than a century of layers with their pentimento stains of breath
and voices before we reach bone, breaking through
plaster holes we patch later, before, at last,

the last wet swaths of our chosen painted shade dry; we finish
in the day's fading gold. This is the work of house
and body. Every decorous self a patchwork

of seams and glue, a mashup of lives to make one. Each accretion,
each wound and scab a making and unmaking, the flesh
a roll of film, a wall of swatches in the shifting

fashions of light. How I've peeled back my own life year into year, hoping
to see the face of the child I was, the one who waits beyond
this last brittle layer of blue, whose shadow

blossomed into this life, this room.
Who blooms through his million lids of sleep, his chorus
of bruise and roses. Who sings and sings: *Be true, be true.*

II.

TETHER OF YEARNING

How it eyed me wildly, sea and idle,
knew me river through. Slipped in on
the gloaming, drowning was floating,

a field for the need-flooding dark.
How it eyed me, blood obsidian,
drift of the moon-hemmed clouds.

Hymn of wind-hum, hymn of sway,
sparking the blood-threading wick.
Seeding the stalk, dew at the tip,

how it teased me summerlong.
How it deftly lipped every cusp.
Caught me with tether, caught me

with web, wanted me song-drawn
and strewn. How it gazed me, saying
soon. Rose as an ocean, blushed

and swollen, breaching flesh and vein.
How it ushered me wildly with tongue.
How it eyed me sweetly—eyed me

and then some, willed me—singing
come. Come coastline mist, come
cotton on a stick, come kiss in the pink

candy light. For want of a God, old ghost
how it eyed me, ripped to be altered
and spun. Pried me with yearning,

whole where it eyed me, reaching me ripe
for the spill. Wild how it knew me—eyed me
for learning. There's nothing as holy as want.

BIRD

With our hands we entered the forbidden world
that runs alongside the world, shutting the curtains
on a June day. Gone: the sun-splashed lawn,
the sprinkler's chirr, the parade of other kids
pedaling past, sweet barbecue smoke and birdsong,
the neighbor's orange cat stalking the wavering
shadows of the maple tree we'd just climbed.
Gone the life we'd known. How much is dream
now, the summer-dimmed room, the house's hushed
voices, we two boys perched on the edge of my bed.
How we stopped our breath to hear the same song
leaping up the branches of our blood, a question
we both wanted to answer. How we slipped, then,
my friend and I, out of ourselves, the bedroom
door closed. In the half dark, how he traced light
onto my smooth legs, a wing in me opening.
Startled by something outside, how we flew
to dress. All caged, thrashing, breathless,
our chests heaving with thrum and flutter, wet
with sky, how we stood at the door, tucking
ourselves in to dive back into the day we somehow
walked in an hour ago. Padding down the stairs,
out into the brash blaze, how our bodies dripped
with shadows. How we paced across the lawn
again, recalling wet grass, the feel of the earth,
squinting to find the ordinary contour of the world.
At the foot of that old tree, how we stood staring,
another lifetime away, forgetting where we'd
come from, a clump of bloody feathers at the root.

BECAUSE YOU NEVER ASKED ABOUT THE LINE BETWEEN

—after Howard Nemerov

You watched her every summer day, the girl
with golden hair, twirl her gleaming whistle
in the lifeguard chair—dreamt she'd smile your way,
wild thrum of a sparrow thrashing in your chest.

Only a short distance from there to a hillside's
slanted breeze-blown grass, where you and a boy touched

each other's skin, feather-fingered in the light between
afternoon and evening. Riding a gradient invisible,

you never asked. You were too young to know
what your want was—or to want to know. Falling, flying,
there came a moment where you couldn't tell.
And then you clearly flew *and* fell.

LITTLE MOON HERO

Little Moon Hero, how you learned.
How you flew moon-big through the house
in your little black cape, your bright face
taped on. How you learned, floating through
that dark, to catch and hold the broken light
and cast it forward, to keep your back to the world.
How each night your little hands would swing
their little hammer at bedtime, knocking
the bright nail of the sun into the sea.
And how, every waking day, you'd fix the night
back onto your face. Little Moon Hero, how you
learned the years. Your cape and mask grown
too small, how you learned to dream, your hands
pressed hard against the sky, trembling to stop
the orbit, to dream the dust of your dead seas
and valleys still invisible. How you learned to lean
into the light. To disappear. To slip beneath
the daily horizon, going down into adolescence,
down into adulthood, down into the dank shed
of yourself, night after night, sawing and sanding
rails and rungs, to hammer your way to the sky.
How you learned the making and unmaking.
How you ground your chalky bones to fit the hole.
Little Moon, how you learned ellipse and turn,
libration and apogee, tipping your axis to still
each wobble, nightly clenching the ripped white hem
of the sea's black blanket over your face. Little one,
little zero. How you wanted to save them all
from falling, to save them from seeing you whole.

SAY EACH DAY YOUR BODY WAKES ANOTHER BODY

inside of you. First fissure, then split,
this body unfurls, lush and heavy-headed

as a blushing peony. Say your outer body
works its world-hands daily to push

this inner body back into some bloody chamber.
Say *shadow*, say *seed*. While one body looks

away, the other slips the latch, rises every hour,
grazing for what it wants. Say each night

your two bodies are bound enemies, locked
in a cell. The inner body beaten and fetal.

The outer, broken-knuckled and sore.
As one body prays with its eyes, one goes

more blind. As one praises birdsong and sea,
an ancient glacier stuffs the other's ears, stops

its tongue. Or let's say instead: one body, one body,
one song, one song. Say one body learns to see

through the other's eyes, feel with the other's skin.
Through night's open window, a few last pulses

of far light, thunder's muted thrum. Wet grass,
the drip of drenched leaves. Say *shameless*,

say *weave*. As sleep comes, you close like petals
in soft milk light, the moon's silk sheet of grace

spilling over your naked bodies. Your fearless
body, your fearless body. Both of them.

AT HOME ONCE MORE

—after James Wright

Before the mirror, my shirt blooms open
and falls. Unbound, I see—as beyond
a pasture—where I've been led
to believe my flesh
has held me, where sin in sinew tensely ripples.
How long has it grazed in me,
this animal gladness, stepping softly, bowing
toward any welcome gaze. But look, I am
no shy wet swan. I've stepped out of this room, out of my body—
broken into blossom.
I can hardly contain my happiness. Tuft of spring,
my wild stem aches and leans
like a delicate wrist,
lifted toward any caress. Twilight bounds, the light breeze moves me.
I sway near wavering willows, slender in tall grass.
A man steps over barbed wire toward me,
leans close to my face. He'd like
to hold me, but can't.
A blessing—suddenly I realize
he sees me as a horse he can touch. My eyes darken with kindness.
I offer my wild mane, my long ear, my taut neck.
But dare not speak.
I know of men like this. There is no loneliness
like theirs.

AXIS AND OAR

The only way into the light beyond the body
is through the body. Nearing this
current, we're closer to being

annihilated by want. This is how
we're drawn: by a flicker of honey light
in a window across a field of deep snow,

by woodsmoke and winter stars, by some
warm amber thrum of a voice.
Animal and shadow, drawn by flame lick,

by salted flesh, by what we cannot touch.
This is the risk of living outside of time, reigned
by blood, a course every river knows.

The pulse of moon and sea. All proximate air
static charged, a frayed edge
of a dying star—the dark and requisite crush

before flashing out. We combust
or we carry a torch inside. Gravity is a question
for those between worlds, asking what

we'd die to answer. At the brink of this, orbit
and undertow, we turn, axis and oar, soaring
toward the coast we know, our haven sky.

THE LOCKLESS WORLD

—answering Frost's "The Lockless Door"

It's been many years
Since I flew from my cage,
(From my room, to be true.)
But what could assuage

One who came out to hide?
To the knock I'd said *Come in*
Then fled. To be without
Whatever's within.

In the world's wider room,
I'm unoccupied.
I've escaped, but a knock
Comes again, as if I'm inside.

How pray away, or home,
What crosses no floor,
Lights no light—the world
With neither window nor door.

Yet *Come in*—I both hear
And say—as I knock,
Altered and full. To answer
Whatever unlocks.

INFINITY ROOM

"Dreamers, they never learn."
—Thom Yorke

Box with a door so being curious

you enter
not knowing eternity

waits to find you

here where
it has always been

if we are able to wander   in between
the pillars of light

are you the one
my song comes through

the fire inside
of winter

of what burns   *Beyond me, beyond you—*

where language slows
near the mouth

of a cave of ice   what will we make
of forever

in a field   of endless selves
of stars   we may still harvest

from the ever-
swallowing dark   inside the mirror

if we believe   we are not captive
                         in this world of rooms

in what
holds us

ever open   if the box I stepped into
                                 was you

NOT YET YOUNG

When you've worn enough of then and soon
and gone so unsewn of the fingering light.
When brittle your heart in bone and blue,
it's time to know by blood through vein
a dream of unravel and ravine.

When here in the day's last seething,
reed-thin note, before the going under
and in-between, the night's unthreading
in marrow and moon, feel away.
There's more good of unknowing

in all of the dark, than in any some
shell bright day. When face of ice
and far, when stone, when sore
of name and answer, when threadbare shroud,
when shard, let fall. Let night undraw

the shore. You're not yet young. Yet this
song of slow erosion and shadow shows
a brighter this that's maybe more all
of a throatpure wish than prayer,
or any brash accretions of sure.

SELF-PORTRAIT AS AN OPENING SCENE

—The Sacrifice (Andrei Tarkovsky, 1986)

Old man, why carry a thin dead tree to the sea's edge,
asking the boy with the wounded throat to plant it.
As if a later blossom might. As if root. As if

the little man is you as a boy, dragging his toy rope.
Lasso or noose. Castoff actor, the past you ask
to resurrect your future's mute. Too late in the world

for spring—soon the last war will whistle over you;
the end will come. The end you've beckoned with nothing
but talk. Somewhere out across the sea—a fallen bomb

you dream as thunder. Down the long road that splits
the frame, the messenger arrives on a bike, who knows you
as boy and man—speaking from the middle of your life.

You shouldn't yearn so for something, he says to the boy
in the man. *You shouldn't grieve so much,* he cautions
the old man in the boy. Weaving dreamy, infinite loops,

he circles you both on the grass, then stops, rubbing
his head, chasing ideas of eternal recurrence. *All my life,*
he says, *going around waiting for something as if I were*

waiting in a railway station. Old man, why not listen
to either of them—this wandering carrier of maps you were
or the mute boy—who, as you talk, ties one end of his rope

to a low branch, the other to the bike's back wheel
for a laugh. As if to say: stop turning. As if to say: stay.
In the beginning was the Word, the messenger shouts,

riding away. *But you are mute, mute as a fish*. You don't
hear him, already offscreen. You're walking toward
your wooden house with burning hands. The final scene.

Somewhere out across the sea, a blooming war.
A war you dream as storm, a storm you dream
as blossom. Pink flames raining in the breeze.

OTHERSIDE

Even your going / let it find you
Even in hiding / find it knows you.
—Perfume Genius

The knowing says there is no wrong,
no lasting wound. The knowing both
threshold and through. The knowing

says sunrise, says seedling. The long
and swallowing earth, the knowing says,
is only a pulse or a blink. *Another dream*

passing, sings the knowing, sings learn
every hurt as a blessing. The knowing
says only become. The knowing guides

you back to your blood, says this is where
you live. The knowing's call is bell
in the fog, is glitter, is flood of ecstatic

and shatter. All is liminal and hum,
says the knowing, the knowing rings
crack the shell. Lets you live between

the notes for now, knowing you're
learning the song. *You are the song itself,*
the knowing would have you know.

Just try to stop the river from flowing,
the knowing sings. There is no keeping,
the knowing says, the river from the sea

when the sea's inside of you. Try leaving
the light, the knowing says, the light
unweaving you. Lie beneath winter fields

and the knowing reaches, with nourishing
root and seed. Release your leaves, long
before summer's end; let wind scatter

all your notes of goodbye. You're never
lost to the knowing, in staying or going,
if you're ever a season away.

III.

OPENING IMAGE

—after Arve Henrikson

Even Spring's early work: operose—

throat-stuck.
Dull light

through shattered green

windows of a long-abandoned factory
in a winter city
no one visits—

a column of sleet
falls through
a hole in the roof
—a slate gray sky.
Something flaps up above

the rusted beams and pillars, broken
chain links, massive iron hooks
on frayed ropes and cables—

everywhere, ghost music

of machines
that once held everything together.

When she comes,

dragging her yellow gown

across grit and glass,
across tufts of feathers and shit—

her voice crackles—at first— a muted trumpet
in the mist

before throwing herself

open—her impromptu aria
a wide beacon sweeping over the stone avenues,
the empty city.

ONE FOR ALL THE NEAR STRANGERS

We were perfect nobodies before you
sat beside me on a bus, or in a crowded lobby,
our names long from being called. Or staring
down a dark tunnel for a late train. You showed me
a sliver of your broken marriage, your mother's lost
memory. Once in a doctor's office waiting room,
I opened my chest, told you stories of my dead
brother and sister. Once we exchanged names
and briefly hiked side by side in a country new to me,
your dog nosing the wet matted leaves for berries,
inhaling lives of others' footprints on this rutted trail.
Sometimes I wonder if we get closer in these brief
shared orbits than we'd get in a lifetime, accepting—
like the long-married—the wide space between us,
our yawns of silence. In a place I can't remember,
stuck in a long line, your parka smelled like baked
bread and rain. I shared some childhood fears:
foxes, tornadoes. You gave me your fear of solitude,
your dream of a small house on the lake. Or that time
we lurched through turbulence, you clenched
the armrest and I wished I could reach only inches
across that dark country between us to hold
your hand. On flights, we've talked for hours.
Later, if we even remember, we might say
I met someone once *by chance,* or *in passing.*
But what does that mean? And why the curious
sting of such little partings? We offer: *I hope our paths*

cross again, sometime, or *give me a shout if you're ever*
passing through. But we know the truth—
as you lift your bag from the carousel, fading
into the cloud of faces you came from. Departing
toward the rest of your life, as I arrive into mine.

PHILADELPHIA ROOFTOP

—for Ross Gay

Warm summer night, the screech-call of a siren, horns bleeding
down an avenue, the skyline's far diamonds glinting. I've long
forgotten whose party it was or why a couple dozen of us were
up there milling around under the blurred stars in pockets of two
or three, beer bottles clinking, glowing baton tips of cigarettes

conducting a chorus of laughter and chatter. Behind blurred
yellow squares in high-rise apartments across the alley,
silhouettes scrubbed dishes or snored in recliners behind
shut blinds, the facing building playing its nightly mosaic
of so many human shows not worth watching. Then, in one

bright room directly across from us, curtains spread wide,
a naked couple lay down, embraced, and began their night's
slow dance. Over the now made-one body of the crowd of us,
an arcing wave of giggles sparked and rippled like static
on a black dress. Someone tried shushing the rest, a few others

clapped, another near me wisecracked about making popcorn.
Across the rooftop, in our instant audience, an itchy shimmer
of sixth-grade sex ed titters slowly stilled. Witnesses to need,
our once patchy wingspan closing, we had become a dark moth
folding into reverence in this one thrown light. A few blocks away,

maybe a man alone in his room watched the dying whir of his
ceiling fan, practiced saying the word *cancer*. Maybe a few floors
beneath his, a woman stared up through the beam of TV light

at a white-hemmed helix rising from her smoke, its twirl stitched
with flashes of the late news showing sheets of ice bigger than

this city plunging from calving glaciers into the sea's frothy bloom,
the unfathomable blue slaking its thirst. Maybe in the gone-silent
siren-light down another street north of here, a mother screamed
over her second shot boy, his blood's widening halo flooding
the sidewalk cracks, a scarlet tsunami rolling toward the coast of her

dry lawn, a cop lowering his gun. Yet there we were, sky-high,
congregated, not wanting to look away for one second from this clean
blessing shared in a bright bed before us, this undressed altar of sweat
and breath and want. What can we do but pray—however we still may—
before this world's flaring wick burns out. Before we fuck it all away.

THE RESTAURANT

—inspired by The Restaurant of Mistaken Orders,
Tokyo, Japan

You remember the time the server placed it
before you: that steaming heap of whatever
the fuck—a dinner you didn't want, a plate
bound for another diner? Then the hasty

apology, the eternal wait. Not to mention,
all the other times—the trauma of no ketchup
bottle, no silverware, hunk of bloody flesh
instead of tofu, or, God forbid, needing to suffer

your momentary thirst, an empty glass glaring
at you. You remember? The sting of injustice,
the sense of being wronged, maybe even
secretly hated by the smiling server, the chef,

the management, the universe. Now, imagine
relinquishing orders. Just taking what you get.
What kind of a world is that? In the dark
corner booth, a man stares for hours at an empty

place setting. Another receives someone else's
dessert. Near the door, a couple grapples
with their marriage suddenly scratched
from the menu. A young mother draws both

of her children close, handed a plate of stage
four cancer, as another leaves, opening their bag

to find a to-go order they didn't place: the dream
job, mansion on the bluff, its glass façade a mouth

filling every evening with the spilled sherbet
of a sunset. And here it comes—at last—your
life, just as you imagined it, perfect and succulent,
trailing a sweet flag of smoke, as it passes you by.

MORNING STAR

—COVID-19 global pandemic

In the world before we knew how near we were
to each, we'd welcome touch. In the world before,
beyond a passing glance or wave, we'd cross the road—
embrace. We'd laugh so hard, we'd gasp. We'd speak
of life beyond our health, unconcerned with measured

breadth. We'd hold each other in small rooms, skin
against skin, inhale the long and languid hours
of an afternoon, never knowing we were strangers.
Before *speed of transfer* and *spread*, before *distance*,
before our bladed breath was blemished mist,

was morning star or mace, we'd dance. We'd kiss.
In the world before the savagery of contact, before
the day was veiled a silver sheen of fear, we'd walk
on narrow paths through woods in dying light.
Standing on the same thick root, behind the pink

and fragrant drapery of clenching vines, we'd pause
and hear each other breathe beneath the breathing trees.
Lovers and friends alike, our voices in passing
were hushed and mingling with dusk. How brave
we were, our mouths so close, before we knew the world

behind a mask. How I'd reach for your hand in parting
in the world before. How I'd reach for your hand,
even now, dear enemy, as I dream us standing there
in the world before the war. Before we knew how
much to care, before the lethal coronation of the air.

VIRAL VIDEO

In a far city the clubs are swinging; one dance
spills out into the street, a pulsing crowd of men
surround a fallen man. Now he kneels as if
prostrate in prayer, evening light flooding
the alley, his white shirt drenched with sweat
as he laughs. Look closer. Not dancing. Not sweat,
but handprints of blood and dirt, the road a red black
pool around him. Don't scroll. The faces caught
above him wear—look closer—not joy, but rage.
If one could swipe the clubs and rocks from their hands
they might be a choir, mouths thrown wide, blessing
a bleeding man with showers of ancient song and prayer.
Hit mute and just like that this moment might be
beautiful, a chorus: God singing through their mouths,
the man on the ground smiling, full of song.
Don't scroll. God sings through the thrown stones
and the song is *Our God refuses your life.*
The song is *Your body is a vessel full of the wrong God.*
Look closer. He's covering his head with his hands
to keep the song out. No, he is crying. He is trying
to keep the blood of his God inside. The blood of his life
from spilling out. *Too late to swipe*, they sing through
my screen, and I click my home button red, lift my head
and touch my son's hand, smudge it with blood.
Blood on my daughter's cheek as I kiss her before
school, her palm wet and red as she hands in
her homework. Blood on her desk and pencil.

On the chalk. On the book she gives a friend.
Blood on the friend's shoelaces. On the basketball
he dribbles, painting red globes across
the wooden floor, a stained mosaic of the bleeding
world. Blood on my steering wheel, my radio dial.
On the dollars I hand to the barista. On the cup
she gives to another. Blood on soup spoon
and bowl, on door handle, light switch, remote.
Blood in the mist. On my tongue and breath.
Wrong God, the millions sing. *Wrong God, Wrong*
God, blood of centuries the soil drinks. Blood in dawn's
wide mouth, in the rusty bell of dusk. *God*, the viral
song of thirst. Blood of God the earth wrings out.

THE HATE PARADE

Miles long, a dragon of honking trucks and flags
drags its burning rubber tail of rage and smoke
through our town. In a van with my kids, grid-

locked at an intersection parking lot, we're forced
to watch it pass. *No more bullshit*, the signs say.
Pro-Life. Pro-Gun. Pro-God. All the drivers

pumping white fists—their wide mouths
spraying flame. Riding shotgun, my oldest reaches
for history: *What would even the worst of our dead*

presidents think, watching this, they say.
Prince of humor and sense, hand on the hilt
of a solid A in AP US Gov, they jab at the beast

with facts: Andrew Jackson, the rise of populism.
But the dragon only rears up louder, howling
at us, at my kids. Ire seething to boil,

I roll down my window to flip off the parade
as it passes, but pause. They're armed, and I don't
want my kids to learn to answer hate with hate.

I raise the window, muting the horns, the hiss of gas.
You should have done it, my daughter says, the pilot
light of her voice flicking at me from the backseat.

A tear on her new eyeliner, she looks away, won't
take my hand for comfort. My daughter, with her
pride pinned to her shirt, her loving heart a deep blue

gem burning through the world, now dim
with hurt. Look what all the lies have ignited—
all those times I told them *There's no such thing*

as monsters. The times I threw on the light
to show them nothing lived in the dark
closet or under their beds. And here it is.

CLEARING THE LOT

Of what he was. A man touches
the stump of what he was

just cutting. And can't see into
himself. Can't hear the missing

song. Of wing and daughter.
Fingers dozens of rings, unfeeling.

All a teeth chain sky of falling.
Hours trembling in a trunk-shaken

house, I watch the saw-men saw
and can't unsee. Growth ache steams

from limbs of a severed morning.
Makes all a falling daughter.

It takes unfeeling men to clear
each lot. Who call her to follow.

To clip her wing by wing. Who pray
her growth to take. To haul her gone.

Plot by plot to prey on limb and branch.
Takes such so-called men of God

to shred and feed. Clear each lot
of girl and song. To swallow.

To undaughter a nation, ring by ring.
And leave a hole. They who mute

her true God heart and gut her throat.
To fallow nation. Who verse by verse

replace her song. Who stuff her world
with empty and follow. So may every mother

come ghost bird home to every daughter.
Girl by girl to lift bright throat. To forest

a future. So may ghost of every mother tree
feed her seed and flight. And bring us song.

MIRROR MIRROR MANIFESTO

Here's the hammer. Here's the nail.
Take your father by the hand.
Raise a nation. Build a wall.

Shut your trap and catch the ball.
Wipe your face off little man.
Swing the hammer. Hit the nail.

Walk it off and never tell.
Hurt in silence. Understand.
It's our nation. Raise the wall.

Take a shovel. Fill the hole.
The land is ours and fear's the land.
Be the hammer. Not the nail.

Grab a drink and drain the well.
Hate the father in your hands.
Build a nation made of walls.

Load the chamber. Lock the cell.
Hide your war. Your private hell.
Be the hammer. Not the nail.
Raze the nation. Build that wall.

USED TO BE A SWEET BOY

The shooter running across the playground,
his bouncing curls, his diaper peeking over
his blue jeans. The shooter's long eyelashes.
The shooter pushed on the swing,
the warmth of his father's hand, big as his back.
The shooter's girlish delight. The shooter
laughing down the bright orange slide,
his mother waving from the park bench.
The shooter in the sandbox watching a pack
of kids run past. The shooter kicking stones.
The shooter opening his lunchbox.
The shooter drawing a portrait in art class.
The shooter's soft cheek in the glow of his
bedside lamp, listening to his mother's moans
on the other side of the wall, her ribs kicked in.
The shooter hearing each dull crush.
The shooter's chin on his soft hands.
The shooter trying to read.
The shooter's finger pulling
the curtain aside to look at the moon.
The shooter behind the wheel of his first car.
The shooter smiling at the cashier,
her shiny red lipstick. The shooter on break,
standing in the alley behind the dollar store, pressing
his back to the sun-warmed bricks. The shooter
staring at the red swipe of a half-drawn circle
around the bright A at the top of his essay.

The shooter alone in the busy cafeteria.
The shooter driving home.
Hair on the shooter's arm riffled by a breeze.
The shooter's black coat on its hanger.
The shooter's face, screen-lit.
The shooter licking an envelope. The shooter
closing a book. The shooter pulling a blanket
up to his chin. Sleep parting the shooter's lips.
The shooter's eyes rolling beneath thin lids.
Tomorrow's active shooter pregnant with dream.

THE DROP-OFF

Dark October morning, the swish and blur
of red brake lights beyond our wipers
as we pull into the drop-off lane. Kids tumble
from lined-up cars and vans like paratroopers

huffing backpacks, lunch bags and instrument
cases under umbrellas, silhouetted in headlights,
marching into school. Every day I say it twice—
I love you, have a good day—I love you—

before you disappear, entering the stream
of bodies flowing into the lobby and halls.
You don't know this: how most days I stall,
blocking traffic, stealing a moment to memorize

the bright facts of your hair, the side of your faces,
to study your walk, caressing your backs
and shoulders with my invisible hand.
Or that I blow you a kiss—like a wobbling globe,

its glassy sheen I dream bulletproof, I dream
impenetrable—floating toward you—to surround
and guide you, my love's great armor to guard you.
This is the same kiss blown by all of history's

moms and dads—look at us in those grainy pictures—
huddled on docks, waving the small flags

of our handkerchiefs at some tiny ship
on the horizon, or watching from our porches

the passing troops, wishing you weren't
in their number, praying you'll never see it
face to face: the angry red slash, the fresh
eraser, the open mouth of the zero.

AMERICA'S GREATEST HITS

cue the breaking news
cue the victim names
cue the gun debate
cue the shooter's aims
cue the bloody hall
cue the flood of memes
cue the *thoughts and prayers*
cue the *broken dreams*
cue the shout for laws
cue the deaf delays
cue the parent shock
cue the stacked bouquets

SHELL AND WING

—for the parents and families of those lost in school shootings

I.

I hold you, breath beneath my skin, a nest of flesh. No world can break
you here. Shadows feather the shell. If you fly, you'll never go far.
I dream my body border and sky, my heart an aviary. In my sleep, you wake.
I hold you. Breathe a nest beneath my skin, flesh no world can break.
Now, the season's errant and astray; coiled rage hisses to strike. Hate leaks
into vine and branch, river and vein. So, song in me, rise. May death take no air
I hold. You, my breath beneath. My skin a nest of flesh. No world can break
you. Here, shadow. Feather, never go. I'm a shell if you fly. Fly far.

II.

You dream you hold me in your nest of breath. Before they lifted me
from mingled blood, I rose, a song within your feathered sleep
for centuries. Your veined branches mapped my lidded eyes. A tree
you dream you hold. In your nest of breaths before me. They lifted me
from you to veil the sky. I flew through your death in learning to fly.
No world bears us. Though we slip our nets of wing and flesh, may love keep
you, this dream you hold in your nest of breath, before they lift me
from mingled blood. I wrote your song within. My feathered sleep.

IV.

THE GREAT VESSELS

—after seeing a photo of "heartstrings" on the internet

Just keep poetry out of it for one goddamn second.
The matter is this: the heart's nothing more than some
humdrum pump, a bloody knot of clockwork. Just ask
the one who slips a silver scalpel into this mess

to save us. No surgeon ever excised love, no harbored
secrets ever spilled onto the cold steel gurney at the end.
It's just an organ. And not the musical kind, either.
Not a drum. Not a compass. Not a fist thumping

freedom, freedom from behind the bony bars. Not
a lonely hunter. It's no lyre or harp. And the so-called
heartstrings? We can blame some heartsore fifteenth-century
sap for that. Here's what's true: the chordae tendineae

do what they do. It's factual. Anatomical. Magnified
by a gazillion, these creamy strands of sinew—
hate to break it to you—just do their daily work:
anchor tendons, keep the canopy open for blood

to flow. And the Great Vessels? That's just another
name for aorta, pulmonary trunk, vena cava (superior
and inferior), the veins—no, not rivers—just keeping
blood moving. But no sooner do I say *anchor*—I begin

to sink into *the blue of my heart, tugboat saving me*
from grief. Can't say *our blood to flow* without wanting

to say *love is every seaward river*, can't see *canopy*
without floating toward *O heart, you blood-red*

parachute—you silky, sky-wide savior. Yes. Silky.
Like that parachute we spread across the fourth-grade
gym floor. No, not a parachute—a giant heart, and Julie
beside me giggling, while we all tug, then lift it high, then

run under it—swallowed by this rainbow jellyfish shot
through with strands of yellow light. But, you see, because
you know how *heartstrings* work—when I said *Julie beside me*
you knew it meant I was crushing hard, that Julie was both

the jellyfish falling over me and the weird ocean swelling
inside me. *Julie*, her bright laugh an enormous diaphanous
dress, a floating-down angel come to rescue me with, yes,
the light in her sad eyes. *Julie* in her Snoopy T-shirt

and pink rain boots. *Julie* the best one in math. You knew
as I began, even now, a lifetime later, to repeat her name
that something in me is still tangled in its fabric, unwound
by even the memory of her voice, that those strands

of yellow light—no, not sunbeams piercing caged gym
windows—were love itself, its search beams sweeping
the sea for souls like us, all of us, the great vessels,
all fray and thrum and ache, and lost as we'll ever be.

SPIN THE BOTTLE

On the gritty cement playground behind the school.
On a garage floor with its world map of oil spills.
On the deck of a vacant house, bikes tossed in the high grass
of an overgrown lawn. Sitting in the dingy summer haze
of someone's bedroom, their door shut even though
their parents weren't home. (The parents were never home.)
Wherever it was, we'd sit on haunches or cross-legged,
close but not touching, waiting for one kid to slip it out
of a backpack like a smuggled treasure. The narrow pop
bottles spun the best. As if we were about to hum
with interstellar vibration, we'd huddle, breathless,
giggling, the air crackling with want and static, *my turn now*,
gripping the bottle's sides like a tuning dial. Whispering
even if we didn't need to, body heat drawing our circle tighter.
From overhead, we were a clockface, each of us an hour
poised to blast into a dizzying future. There's a hand, ready
to spin. There we are, leaning away from its stiff aim,
hoping it won't, hoping it *will* stop on us. One is licking pink
glossy lips, one tucks a wavy curl behind their ear, another's
delicate fingers pull at tube socks under bare knees.
Bumpy with initial friction, now our spin hums like an anti-gravity
vortex. When it stops, it's going to point to someone I'm going
to kiss, and we're going to kiss with everyone watching.
Check out the blur of the tapered neck, its sugary mouth blushing
into a high-pitched gasp, its moan deepening into a full-throated O.
If we've spun it just right, with all the other kids
spinning bottles tonight around the world, all these frenzied

glowing whisks, it will spin forever, plunging its glorious tongue
of light up through the O-zone, a giant obelisk probing the deepest,
neediest reaches of space. Imagine all the wet lips coming together
around the earth if we keep it spinning. If we keep it spinning,
soldiers everywhere dropping their weapons, turning to kiss
whoever's beside them, the whole war itself even, suddenly nude
and slipping into the nearest river at dusk. Strangers leaning
across checkout lanes, some getting their tongues involved.
Teenagers everywhere—well, obviously. But the octogenarians,
the nonagenarians, too. And look, up there, if we can just keep
it spinning, two astronauts, peering through their rocket window,
saying *Look at all the sweet fucking light of the Earth*, undressing,
their spacesuits and underthings orbiting them as they kiss.
If we keep it spinning, they'll release their lips for one second
that will feel like hundreds of years to watch the night lawns
and houses lifting off the lonely earth, the gray-suited
accountants and parents floating past, the bikes and cars
and coffins, the guns and the wars, and even our bottle gliding
past their ship like a Catherine Wheel, spitting slow-motion sparks.
And look—there goes two of us, our cheeks just barely touching
like two fuzzy peaches in a bowl, floating toward the Milky Way,
all of it spinning onward, wet and electric, millions of humming,
glowing bottles floating off the earth like new galaxies, spinning
toward the glorious, tender, original sucking and blowing of never
into forever, into the one, the final and eternal, ever-loving smooch.

GARDEN CELLO

Come we swarm to the sun-warmed gold.
Come we to the wood, come we drawn
to hum and hold. Come we lonely. Come we low.
Come we pray to key and scale, to homilies
of thrum. Come we sonata. Come we want.
Come we to bowed head and scroll, come we
spiral round the blooming bud. Come we curl
and thrill. Come we pulse of the bow's slow lick.
Come we flow. Come we tease the hem
of purfling, come we drone and purr. Come we
down long neck and waist. Come we finger,
come we peak. Come we glide vibrato. Come we
itch to crest and spill. Come we tongue and blossom.
Come we solo, come we cell. Come we call
and follow. Come we cavity. Come we dive.
Come we honey stomach. Come we nectar melody.
Come we alive. Come we to the F-hole gates,
come we to the sweet dark hive. Come we
crescendo. Come we full and hollow. Come we
whole and home. Come we come we honeycomb.

EPITHALAMION IN RETROSPECT

—for Denise, including lines from "Born to Run"

Let's go where the wind goes, back
to that August night: Atlantic mist,
Jersey coast, boardwalk Ferris, bold
and stark through veils of fog, mad

gulls wheeling over the ever-pulsing
cascade, teeming shrieks of a delighted
hour. Let's soar above the breaking sea
that carries and careens such teen souls

as these, as ours, together. Oh, the runaway
American dream: Here comes a girl
with a lit match. Here comes a boy
with a wooden heart. The rest, as they say—

yes—but all history, every diamond nova
born and fading begins with this blaze.
Every everlasting kiss. Do you want
to know love is real? Look at us there,

far grown near, face to face for the first
time, hands trembling, lost in the glow
of each other, birds sprung from cages,
huddled on the beach in the mist.

What could we have known of a future
we were making, of two later souls

being born through us. Dark sky heart,
even before your name burned in me

that night, I knew—we're gonna get to
that place where we really want to go.
Years on, now—if ever our star dims,
near grown far, scared and lonely riders,

I want to die with you. Let's go where
the wind goes. We can live with the sadness.
You want to know love is wild? Look at me.
Let's run. Velvet, glory, mansion, let me in.

THE BOX

Graced with a faded map of the ancient world
and wrapped with an old rubber band, it sits
on the dresser within arm's reach of our bed,
this box we bought years back in the knick-knack
aisle of a home décor shop. It's close to the size
of an airplane's black box, which, says the internet,
resists crash impact of more than 300 miles an hour
and contains an underwater locator beacon
called the "pinger." Just think of that tiny
ultrasonic *ping*, that star blinking up through
the ink-black sea from the shattered tail of a plane
gone lost. Is love a form of data? Remember how
it felt—we two teenagers with an entire sky
between us, me in Michigan, you in Pennsylvania,
penning letters longer than ten pages—crushing
distance with ink and paper? I remember the gulf,
the plummet, then crash—the maw of an empty
mailbox on days no letters came. And when they did,
what holy ascent, how I'd float on the jet stream
of your blue cursive for hours, dream you close.
Now long-married, drifting in comfortable silence,
or busy, we can go days saying less than a page.
Or—turbulence, storm—days we barely speak,
nights we lie like capped pens on a white sheet.
Yet as we sleep, there it is—*ping, ping, ping*—
this box of our letters, just one stack, dozens more
in the attic. If we go missing, let the searchers come.

Let them sweep our sea for signs—in all
the heartsick mush and mundane glory of a couple
kids, new as we were at navigating the heights,
scratched into analog. Let them find us by our words.

VERTEBRAE

"By now if you are not my true topography, / then what?"
—Katie Hartsock

That you love what is broken and you bring it home.
Back from the ocean, you open swaddled treasures,
place them before me: a spine in pieces across

our kitchen counter. Where does this lead, this lost
cartography. We read the blackened shadows
of vertebrae, each a word of a story long missing:

fin, fluke and limb. Of what was a swimmer, a wet
and muscled fish, once fluid and filled with sea-song.
With tongue. Even in speaking, shifting sands

of language bury us. If wrought hollow, every bone
we speak is echo, is snapped branch, is ancient hub.
The discs between—what once was whole—etched

like Aztec carvings, faces of a sun God, cartilage
of vein and sea. That you unearthed what lay
for years unseen. That you give me one vertebra, a souvenir

for my writing desk. A fragment I hold to reach the depths,
the poem. A distant sea. Am I dolphin enough to dream
my way through us. Through you. Where are we halo

of salt and silence. How long have we lain separate
and dry. How do we endure such desiccation, such
unwoven dark. What draws us close ruins us. Even now,

I can't escape the current sentence, need the story
          conjugal and whole, want this bonded, sinuous,
a column for blood and light. Want grace again.

Who will find us here, dropped as we are like branches.
          What is left of every heart is reliquary. Is this:
now you hold it up to my eyes—a trace, a filigree,

an etching feather-light as air, where nearby tendrils
          have slipped between the discs as if to map
the architecture, frail arteries for some later pulse

to nourish us whole. Evidence of a world grown
          around us, of what we've made. May we be
tree again. May this be root of how you once found me.

TROUGH

"Desire is the cool water sloshed / into a trough at dawn."
—Aimee Nezhukumatathil

Is the distant silver curtain of rain,
long in coming. Is shimmer and oasis.
Is prayer. Is beam in the dark.
Is the needling gleam. Is glance
and shoulder. Is white filigree curtain
riffling. Is one ripple becoming a wave
in the open sea. Is crest and curl.
Is cool sheet. Is lemon. Is mint.
Is the tipped pitcher. Is tumbler.
Is caress. Is sweat on the glass.
Is the moonlit window. The night
laid out before us. Is deep green
and shadows. Is secret bower.
Is a field of tall grass at midnight.
Is spill. Is slake. Is high tide.
Is tongue and vein. Is hip and haunch,
is quivering sinew. Is biting the lip.
Is thirst at the root. Is jasmine.
Is moonflower. Is the night wind
finally reaching the woods.
Is tall trees slow dancing. Is making
our way to the floor. Is step and glide.
Is tomorrow a world away.
Is kissed throat and palm. Is moan.
Is rain on the roof, the filling trough
of dawn. Is no going back.
Is *here* answering *where*.
Is *now* answering *when*.

THE UNSPEAKABLE

The unspeakable spoken and spoken until it becomes
bladed ball, burning star in your throat, spit
toward dark. A tattered eyeless doll's split
blue seam, stuffed clouds blooming from

a ruptured sky. Every careful hem you knit
with love undone. Deep mouth leviathan, song
of keen and ache—now your fat slick tongue's
a slit whale, the bloody deck a spill of *holy shit.*

So is every hole from *whole* unsewn and seen.
Let this gush be oil. Be light for a million lamps.
Be fuel. Be seed. Be skyward vine from cramped
earth, bare feet crushing your dark berries into wine.

THE MOSAIC CHAIR

From another room, you hear me drop
a plate or mug or glass or bowl, and wince,

gasp, laugh. This daily shatter has become
our soundtrack, and me, the grand composer

of this symphony of crash and ruin.
Who could love such a clumsy lunk,

such a bumbling klutz clomping through
the world, so dumb-fisted. I mean this

literally—who could love me: my periphery
black ice for miles, a train of wreckage

all the way to the horizon—a river
of glint and sliver. And the sky over me?

Millions of new dishes tumbling
in slow motion, forever. A falling future.

Answer? You. You, who saves every fragment,
every smashed piece. Who I watch

this spring morning through our kitchen window
as you smooth damp plaster

onto the seat of an old metal garden chair
        setting each bright shard into a circle,

something broken you make whole,
        as I lift another dish with wet hands.

ON THE NAMING OF THINGS

"We must unlearn the constellations to see the stars."
—Jack Gilbert

As we walk in autumn woods, a winged flame
chitters and drips from branch to branch, some
peripheral flash we try to catch but can't.

It's flown, this beautiful luminous whatever
it was—gone. Yet here we stand, scanning
the sky as if it will return, like a word

we can't quite remember. Which it doesn't.
But which does have a name: *lethologica*—
that tip-of-the-tongue phenomenon. Who knew?

And don't ask me how I still know that
pink-fringed hulk of mist drifting above us
is called a *cirrocumulus*. Anyway, what

difference now—*cardinal, tanager, flicker, finch.*
We argue this from time to time: if the essence
of a thing is lessened or lost, given a name.

You say: never—that we see it better, once
identified. I like to say I'm not so sure, even if
I half believe it. There, across the river,

see that sequined dancer quaking in the field,
that silver ghost outside the crowded pines?
I loved that tree so much more before I learned

its blinding name. Look at *us,* after all.
Most of our lives I've walked beside you,
a shadow flitting through my inner branches.

When it finally settled in a clearing, I gave it
a name. Now I look out through its eyes,
I'm all you see. And all you'll never see again.

EVENING AT HIDDEN BEACH

—Lake Superior, Marquette, Michigan

I'll never forget your laugh as we broke the dark
with our hands, the lake's flat sheen sparked
into diamonds—a shower of glitter. We splashed

in shallow waves beneath a mottled gray, ashy
clouds allowing the sun only fleeting peeks,
the way a transient flame from embers leaps.

We keep so much inside. Nearing sunset, we watched
the sky's wool quilt retreat for good and cheered—
the coast's tall pines, the jutting cliffs instantly

blazing, everywhere dripping with big gold light.
It's easy to recall the surface of a day—the brief
flash any picture catches—how we swam and laughed,

our hearts ignited by sudden light. But that day's
treasure lies deeper. Let's look again, down through
the glassy green and amber, past silver scattering

flakes of minnows. Do you remember those stones,
the ones they call *yooperlites*? How they'd glare
in murky silt and we'd gasp at their passing beams.

Like beacons on the lake floor, gleaming from
the inside. On this winter morning, I hold one
of those dull gray stones we kept, heavy

as an antique coin. Nothing flashy about it. A cool
smooth cloud flecked with tiny white stars that seem
too many miles away to dazzle a world into day.

But you and I know better. Why hold such a blaze
and not show it always? Yes, the heart is more
like that, remember. The heart is more like that.

WATCHING YOUR DAUGHTER WALK TOWARD LOVE

and suddenly she is five again, and here it comes—
                    a falling wall of dark water to swallow her
          as you dive to catch her hand.

Though it was calm, then—remember?
                    Each lapping wave just a soft lip
          at her feet. But you should tell her,

she who is now as tall as you—
                    love's a wild sea that won't show
          its true depth until an undertow

clutches her breathless in its fist, in currents
                    fierce enough to shuck any spirit
          from its shell. You must tell her

with all the rivers in the blood—run, no, don't,
                    or yes—run—wide-armed right into,
          or no—far from this tidal crush.

Watch now as she wades into the other
                    world, squinting into spindrift and mist
          at what you cannot see, willing a serpentine

pull, the roil beneath. Look—she's too far out,
                    waist-high in its deep mouth, your voice
          muted by wind, by distance she needs

from you. Trust the ocean in her
                    knows you—knows the coast in you
          goes nowhere. Have you forgotten, father?

Remember, without you
                    having drowned in the arms
          of such bliss, the thunder of such

sweet foam and thrash, she wouldn't
                    be here, this soul-bright fish, leaping farther
          and farther now—and now gone under.

MORNING ELEMENTS

—Carp Lake, Michigan

Through a parted cottage curtain at sunrise
I watch the German widower and his boy,

two silhouettes holding hands at the edge
of the lake's emerald mirror. Last night

in a circle of strangers and friends at the beach
campfire, he spoke of his wife's death a month ago,

how he chose to travel across America with his son
for the summer. In shadow, his smile flickered,

that brief, brave smile the mourning offer,
seeing through the rest of us—through the world—

the way I imagine he and his son do now, looking
beyond the glassy water before them, this wide

future, wraiths of backlit surface mist caressing
their chests and shoulders as they sink, one step

then another, shivering into another element, resonant
silver circles ringing from their bodies as they disappear.

STRANGE MUSIC

"From the time I let go till the moment I strike the water everything is blank, and my ears have filled with strange songs."

—Harry Houdini

There's never been such a song as stay—
The world is always falling away.

The river's ever-going tone
Is full of far—a draining, sea-drawn
Moan. *Be near,* the moon drones on,
And gone. A song such as this never stays.

Even bridges sway. A song of gusts aching
Rivet and beam, the cable-breaking
Strain as I sleep. The leap is waking
Through. I'm a world always falling away.

There's never been a song such as stay
In a world of always. Falling away

Is all I hear. The current rushes
inside. A deep crescendo crush
To fill the momentary hush.
There's never been such a song as stay.

As I let go, strange music arose—
The only song the body knows:
Nothing holds. Forever flows
always. From a world of falling away.

V.

for my mother—
Mary Kay Fanning

April 13, 1931 – July 28, 2022

BOATS

It's like we're floating out to sea
in a small boat together—
I text my sister, of these hours with you,

hospital curtains closed on the light.
Or maybe I'm in this alone, looking
over the hull for you in a night river:

your mind's usual flash down to a flicker
in the current. In a week you'll be dead
but I don't know this yet. As you sleep,

I watch a row of people cross the dry bed
of the Mississippi on my screen.
The river's drained enough by drought

they walk to Tower Rock, a butte
accessible only by boat—before today.
Why are there so many babies here,

you ask later, pointing at the empty bed
across from yours, squinting at me
for an answer. I don't know if what

you see in the space between us
are spirits or a memory of your own
eight infants. But I want to remember

how to believe in this: in the body as mere
vessel, in a soul that bears us brightly
forward. That when you're gone, if only

by way of a dream (my feet sinking in deep
black mud, you in a nightgown on a far coast)
I'll cross any wide ravine to reach you,

and you'll hold me until morning, until
a flood of light returns to carry me back
to a world gone dark without you.

THE HUNGER STONES

The summer of your dying the Earth was all thirst.
Rhine, Loire, Yangtze, Danube, Colorado, Rhone—
global currents slowed to parched beds. From space,
their desiccated channels whittled into brittle twigs.
Long submerged relics rose from drained rivers

for weeks: Buddha statue, sea henge, lost city,
dinosaur tracks, Nazi warship leaning in the muck,
body of a girl long missing. Everywhere, closed cases
reopening, historians rushing into drained depths,
reading etched warnings of starvation and drought

on hunger stones. You always said you weren't
afraid to die, you just didn't want to die of thirst,
the way you thought you saw your aunt go.
But I've since learned that when swallowing ceases,
it's not thirst or starvation, only our cells done

with being nourished. Sitting vigil beside your bed,
my long-dry faith would have me believe the water
of your being will flow to another sea, that your body
before me is only relic in the making. Only bones:
these hands, these shoulders, your hip like a hillside

jutting from white sheets, your veins becoming
more visible as you near death. It's called *mottling*,
the hospice nurse told me—a word I kept hearing

as *marbling*. We need such good stone words, such
polished words, to make dying sound beautiful.

Beneath the surface of your flesh this *marbling*
like a shadow of bare branches on snow—
tributary, rivulet—your last letter's indecipherable
bleedthrough. A prayer for us in blue script,
flowing, ancient, and to be answered elsewhere.

SHARK WEEK

In the dim of my mother's dying room, as if
bobbing with her on the snapped plank of a ship
far from any coast—my brothers and I try to keep
our heads from swimming, however we can.
Lying on the floor, I watch a shadow's slow blade
slice though our family pictures on her wall
as she floats in waves of morphine under a sheet.
Mike sits at Mom's desk, lost in his phone's glow.
John kicks back in Mom's blue recliner watching
divers plunge one by one off the back of a bright
vessel into black water. I'm pissed he's distracting
himself—and me—with TV, when our mother
is in her last hours. I don't want to hear it, that these
monstrous "gods of the deep" have poor eyesight
and no sense of color, that we're not their prey.
I ask him to mute the volume. *Fish-out-of-water*
breathing is what they call it in the hospice booklet,
her cheeks now flapping loosely like she's gasping.
Tonight, the so-called *death rattle* has begun.
To keep from drowning in the sound, I close
my eyes, remind myself the rattle is in her throat,
not mine, and that it's not hurting her. I imagine
each deep gurgle as something else, like maybe
she's just taking that best final sip of a milkshake
through a straw. Then I settle on the image of
an old metal percolator, like the one she'd pull out
for parties. Yes, it must be just the sweet, dusky music

of coffee burbling in a machine, the gentle sound
of a party winding down. I open my eyes in time
to catch the silver tank, tangled tubes, panic of bubbles,
a diver thrashing free. *Well, you're about to be*
fucking toast—my brother says to himself out loud,
the way I'd forgotten he used to when we were kids,
as if people on TV could hear him. Need a mood
ripped to shreds? Leave it up to John. But then again,
thank God for him—here I was, trapped in its path,
and John snatched me from its teeth, enough time
to breathe as it glides away from this room, swallowed
by the night sea outside Mom's window, leading us
to believe it's gone, not that it's only taking
a wider berth, that it will soon be circling back.

VIGIL

One summer dawn, days after my birth,
you woke to see a stranger dressed in black
standing outside your bedroom's tall open
window, looking through the sheer white
curtain lifting and falling over me in the crib.
You screamed to chase him off, then
screamed again. What chilled you most,
you'd tell me, every time you'd
tell me the story, was how he didn't move.
Just kept staring—turning so slowly

before leaving. So slowly, before leaving,

dusk now bruises into night. Sitting beside
your bed as you sleep, I close my eyes,
cherish your breath as it lasts. I don't want
to see what's coming. What's already here.
At your window, a dark thing knocks
its wings, pressing its face against the glass.
Mother, how long had he stood there
watching us sleep? What blood, what prayer,
what light does he want to swallow—
this thief, this mute priest, this nightlong moth?

SYLVIA

Of course, I'd think of Plath
every time I'd see her—
that lanky, black, sweet old cat

at New Hope Assisted Living,
who'd lie, draped across the couch,
or curl like a shadow in a patch

of sun, watching residents come
and go, pushing walkers or squinting
out windows for hours, at distances

only old eyes can measure.
You couldn't stand her, or any cat,
keeping your door shut all day long,

even though Sylvia, like most
women around you, knew soon
to keep her distance, entering only

the rooms of those who'd give her love.
One afternoon, as we sat out on
the back deck, you scoffed like

a slighted girl as Sylvia padded toward
us, leaping up into my welcome lap.
Long before your eyes began to fade,

you couldn't see her, never able to look
at anything dark or anything you didn't love.
When you entered hospice, suddenly

Sylvia couldn't stay away, standing
on her hind legs, scratching at your
closed door for days. Every night, she'd

sit in the hallway, peering into the strip
of light beneath. As if she sensed it was
your time to go. Leave it to Sylvia to know.

GO, GENTLE

—after Dylan Thomas

Let all your gentle brightness go with age
where all our ages go. Mother, goodnight.
The dying light is gone. You needn't rage.

You knew that every sky was one more page
your lightning words would cross. Without a fight—
let all good gentle brightness go. With age,

good women never fail. They take each stage
to dance. At last, give one frail wave in spite
of dying light. It's gone. Do not rage

at the wild sun's flight, nor try in vain to cage
the hours left to sing. You sang despite.
You let your gentle brightness go with age.

From birth there is no blind, no camouflage;
a woman holds the grave within her sight.
In dying, a light is born. I will not rage

or weep. Let memory be heritage,
your life my carried lamp against the night.
Let all your gentle brightness go with age.
The dying light is gone. You needn't rage.

WHEN IT IS TIME

We lift the feather box
my wife placed under your bed

during hospice. She lays
a long white eagle feather

on the sheet over your sleeping
chest, a gray heron feather

along the length of your legs.
Bowing over you, I open

my arms wide, rest my cheek
on your belly, my first sky.

BOY IN THE CLOUDS

Stiff and solemn in my charcoal suit, I watch
a boy about four in front of me, flapping as he leaps
from one pale yellow cloud to another, chased by

what looks like a black orb. Looking over his
shoulder, I watch until all the prayers around us
hush to a far hum. He's virtually gone, until, bored,

he swipes off the game, plops his mom's phone
face-down on the pew, tugs at her black dress,
his father's black pantleg. They don't notice, so he

leaps back into the sky he holds in his hands.
I, too, look down at the world I'm supposedly in
to see what's real: the shiny black shoes I seem to be

standing in, haloed by blue stained-glass light,
how it seems I'm falling through a portal in the church's
marble floor. I get his urge to fly. It's hard for any of us

to be here. And what does any of this mean to this kid—
these droning dirges and sniffles—in this moment
he won't even remember. In fact, he won't remember

his great-grandfather, either, my uncle, my mother's
brother, who we're praying for this morning, his ashes
over there in a silver box beneath his cursive name.

To him, the winged boy—leveling up and up and up—
is far more real. *He may no longer be here with us,*
but his new life is just beginning, the priest says.

I close my eyes and remember only weeks ago,
my mother's hand in mine, light as a sparrow, hours
before she died, how hard I fought against the thought

that soon she'd be just a thought. Despite that, I think of her
and feel her arm around my hip tugging me
closer, the way she would when I'd stand beside her

in that drafty stone church, and here we are again,
my mother and her boy, soaring beyond reach of all shadows,
flapping, flapping, flapping, flapping, flapping.

THE CARRYING

A few days after you've died, I dream
I carry you in a car seat into a restaurant.
As the server takes my order, you coo
beside me, entranced by your fingers,

your strange new voice. Back in the waking
world, I've started talking to you, sharing
mundane details of my days. It felt
foreign at first, not knowing if the silence

was translating me, or if you're even listening.
I close my eyes so you can hear me better.
In the quiet infancy of your death,
I imagine you watching each word

spill from my lips, the way I must have
studied each sound falling from your mouth
when I was your baby—all those little black
seeds with poems curled up inside them.

NO MOM, TODAY?

—our favorite waitress asks, approaching
our booth at the usual lunch place.
After I tell her you died last week,
she chokes up and steps away.
I couldn't bear to look across
our table to where you used to sit,
so I slid into your spot instead,
taking in your view for the first time.
And there it is, my empty chair,
the absence I was then to you
all those days you'd talk as we ate
and I'd barely respond, too busy
or tired or blind with self to listen.
Today, across the dining room,
a man sits with his little girl.
She's chatting away, telling some
great story. She reminds me of you,
the way her hands flutter, conducting
a whirlwind of bright notes—
like she's reaching right into
her heart, tossing fistfuls of glitter
at him, as he blindly scrolls
and scrolls. I want to walk over,
smack the phone out of his hand.
We only get so much time.
I want to shout it in his face.
We only get so much time.

AFTER YOUR DEATH I TRY TO LEAVE MY BODY

The only thing I wanted was your rosary,
that blue garland of gems, sacred worry beads
you turned and turned, praying as you looked

into framed faces of your children. If only
to feel each decade still warmed by you.
Vehicle, *Vessel*—watching your body fade,

I kept thinking of those words. Days later,
in a parking lot, the funeral home's
Certified Cremation Services Provider

handed you over to me in a plastic box,
your ashes the lightest, heaviest thing
I've ever held. So this is how it is.

We're less than breath, but more
than bodies. In those first days
of missing you, I wanted religion

again, to be guided as you were, by reins
of faith and ritual. I hung your rosary
from a hook above my bedroom window

where it sways and glints. This morning
I lie on my bed watching translucent cells
twirl across my walls, a bead-thrown galaxy

orbiting like a disco ball's spun stars.
        God, forgive me—the parched grass
                of my flesh ever asking fire, my hollows

craving deluge and fill, the thrill of a good hard
        rain. Forgive me want, my blood's wild
                dancer, her scarlet dress. Forgive me

need's unceasing pulse, the spin that wakes the veins'
        urgent circuitry, one thrown switch and all
                my night cities sparked to life.

Forgive me desire's inextinguishable prayer.
        Or maybe—do not. Maybe this urge, this ache,
                this eternal plea for touch, is all I have to answer.

FLASHLIGHTS

Putting the last of your belongings into boxes
and bags, I find them—all the lost, cheap plastic
flashlights I bought as your world grew dimmer.
Flicking one on, I point it onto dusty carpet
in the empty corner where only days ago you lay
in a bed. I was nine the year you first gave me
this gift of light. Under my sheet that Christmas
night, I switched on my new blue flashlight's
wide beam, lit the hidden world alive. I loved
dreaming its pale circle on my ceiling a portal
or passing my hand through the dust-flecked shaft.
Or my favorite trick: slowly smothering the lens
to cringe as some giant's dark hand reached down
through the sky of my ceiling. And how it lit
a miracle of blood and bone inside my hand:
red vines twined across my knuckles' shadowy
branches, the whole tree in me suddenly visible.
I never told you how later I'd seethe each time
you'd reach into your box of bulbs to pull out
Jesus, the Light of the World. Or *Look toward*
the light, or some other snuffed metaphor
to keep me from looking too long at the dark.
Now: the box in my arms literal, the dead bulbs
literal, and me dying to see your bright face
tell me, just once more, of all the light in our hands.

EXPIRATIONS, EASTER

We want you back reads the light
blue script on the subscription card
for *A Simple Life* magazine.
Your membership notice for AARP
is here again, too, second time

this week they're here to remind you:
you've expired. The world wants you back
to pay your dues. Even that shitty hospital's
still looking for thousands for pumping you
with useless fluids and pills, and here's

the bill for your last ride in an ambulance,
now gone to collections. On my desk
a growing stack of envelopes sits,
sealed and crisp, abstract rectangles,
your name watching me through

the windows. Outside my window here,
the sun's nothing but a white hole
in thick mist, a foggy Easter morning.
The first you've missed since—look how
I say *you've missed*—as if you forgot,

as if calendars and holidays still matter.
Now, from a couple blocks away, the clanging
bronze call to mass peals through the gauze.

Remember a few years ago, you and I
walking in that stream of bonnets and blazers

into Sacred Heart? You'd only just begun
to ask me something when the carillon's
thunder, right over us, nearly shook us
from our skins, catching you mid-question.
I turned in the mad crash of bells to see you,

film-star glamorous in your white scarf,
your red horn-rimmed shades, the skyward
lily of your face trumpeting with mute, shaking
laughter, the perfect answer you often gave
to the world and its clamorous demands.

LIFE'S WORK

For decades you spoke of it—the book
you'd soon begin to write. Mother of eight,
your first six all adopted—each chapter
would be about one of us. Doctors, waitresses,
any strangers within earshot heard the synopsis
over the years. The story shimmered from you,
page after blank page falling like gold leaves
onto the surface of a glinting river, only never
into ink. Every home you lived in had a "writing
nook," a corner desk with pens and sharpened
pencils in a cup, framed covers of your favorite books
on the wall, two wrapped reams stacked like bricks
on the shelf. For years I tried to spark you to start—
we knew Oprah'd snatch it up, knew anyone
who'd hold it would be changed. *A Little Book
of Love* was the last of many titles you tried out
on me only weeks before you died. Taking my hands,
you leaned in and said its name—and, as if you could
see your life's work appear, you read my eyes.

LAST MASKS

Running an errand, I scrounge in the glovebox
for a Covid mask. Putting it on, it hits me instantly,
that sad pink of your foundation, your lipstick's
fading red aroma. This must have been the mask
you wore the last time we went shopping or to lunch,
or when I drove you to the hospital. Beneath the fabric
of this poem, I want to say I shook with tears then,
doubled over in a crowded parking lot. Because I did—
even though I didn't—in the blur of rushing into
the post office, just before they closed. Standing in line,
I shut my eyes, inhaling you, seeing my face pressed
to yours like it was only hours before you died.
Your gaunt cheeks drawn, your close breath mingling
with mine in the dark, I began to tell you a secret.
I want you to know all of me, now, Mom—I said.
One utterance, only air between us, yet how strange
to hear this buried universe of burn and hurt
flash into being, then flicker out. And that was it.
Before your soul's last drift, the gauzy lift of your
going, a fold of silence where words once were,
the way a veil of clouds reveals the momentary stars.

VI.

ALL WE ARE GIVEN WE CANNOT HOLD

Whirling axis, spine of a spinning top. Love
between us all maybe and blush. Night we press
against us, secret we caress, word we write in steam

we breathe on glass. What we let fly from our fingers,
love between us. String we find to weave a world.
Valleys of lavender spilling for miles. All the stars

we can name. Lemon and willow, love between us.
A riffle of yellow. Shadow of sheets on the line.
Mast and sail, the days adrift, the summer all billow

and cream. Endless *yes*, love between us, and passing.
A drooping flush pink bloom at noon. Love between us
a dappled garden shade, gate of vines. A house of hours

and only we've the key. Love between us the daylong
rain. Love between us glance and veil, the gauzy
sleeve of evening giving way. Gray mare in the mist,

acres of breeze and beachgrass, love between us
chasm and sea. Flicker or blaze. Weather of our making.
Wild heaven going, love between us. All the windfall

apples and the sweet crush of dusk. Love between us
the unfleshed glow. Night a book we want to open,
love between us, the story we writhe inside. Box of letters

in a dusty attic, the sky's ancient fires we extinguish
each day we don't kiss. Static and stir, a spark, love
between us, the silver arc we make across the stark and vast.

Given one life to remember, love between us, one lost
language we're given to taste. Each fading sentence
to erase, love between us. Or to pass between our tongues.

ACKNOWLEDGEMENTS

Grateful acknowledgement and thanks are extended to the editors of the following journals, in which some of these poems first appeared, sometimes in earlier versions:

"All We Are Given We Cannot Hold," *The Common*
"Bird," *Off the Coast*
"Body of Work," *Michigan State University Libraries, Short Edition*
"Clearing the Lot," *One*
"Evening at Hidden Beach," *The Indianapolis Review*
"Garden Cello," *THRUSH*
"Inarticulata," *The Common*
"Infinity Room," *Red Wheelbarrow*
"Little Moon Hero," *Off the Coast*
"Model Nation," *Cutleaf*
"Not Yet Young," *Marrow Magazine*
"On Crater Trail," *Cutleaf*
"On the Naming of Things," *Red Wheelbarrow*
"Opening Image," *Sienna Solstice*
"Philadelphia Rooftop," *Waxwing*
"Say Each Day Your Body Wakes Another Body," *The Baffler*
"Self-Portrait as an Opening Scene," *Parish Line Press*
"Shark Week," *The Indianapolis Review*
"Shell and Wing," *The Midwest Quarterly*
"Snow and Roses," *Cutleaf*
"Tether of Yearning," *The Midwest Quarterly*
"The Drop-Off," *Waxwing*
"The Lockless World," *Porter Gulch Review*

"The Restaurant," *Red Wheelbarrow*
"The Thorn Birds," *The Midwest Quarterly*
"The Unspeakable," *Cider Press Review*
"Used to Be a Sweet Boy," *Gulf Coast*

In addition, I am grateful to Ron Mohring, editor of Seven Kitchens Press, for publishing my chapbook *Prince of the Air*, which includes the following poems from this collection: "Tether of Yearning," "Strange Music," "The Lockless World," and "Say Each Day Your Body Wakes Another Body."

"Shell and Wing," "The Thorn Birds," "Model Nation," and "Body of Work," appear on *All We Are Given We Cannot Hold* (Blue Griffin Records, 2023), an album by composer David Biedenbender. Permission for use of this book's title was given by the author.

NOTES

The title "Tether of Yearning" references a song by Hammock, on their album *Universalis* (Hammock Music, 2018).

The first line of "Tether of Yearning" is from the poem "[Horse] [Buzz] [Carbine]" by Dennis Hinrichsen, from *This Is Where I Live I Have Nowhere Else to Go* (Grid Books, 2020).

The title "The Thorn Birds" references a novel by Colleen McCullough.

The title "Used to Be a Sweet Boy" references a song by Morrissey, on his album *Vauxhall and I* (Sire/Reprise, 1994).

"Infinity Room" is inspired by the artwork of Yayoi Kusama, as well as the song "Daydreaming" by Radiohead on their album *A Moon Shaped Pool* (XL Recordings, 2016), from which it borrows a line. In addition, it takes inspiration from the song's video, directed by Paul Thomas Anderson.

The poem and the title "Opening Image" are inspired by a song of the same name by Arve Henriksen, from his album *Chiaroscuro* (Rune Grammofon, 2004).

"Garden Cello" owes gratitude to a June 28, 2019, BBC story about Professor Martin Bencsik, who donated his cello to provide a hive for 20,000 bees in his garden.

"Epithalamion in Retrospect" weaves in lines from "Born to Run" by

Bruce Springsteen, from his album *Born to Run* (Columbia Records, 1975).

"The Unspeakable" begins with a line by Keetje Kuipers from her poem "Blackfoot River," from *Beautiful in the Mouth* (BOA Press, 2010).

GRATITUDE

Thank you: Steve Gillis, Michelle Dotter, Dan Wickett, Chelsea Gibbons, and all at Dzanc Books for believing in this collection.

Thank you to all my wonderful students at Central Michigan University, and to my colleagues, especially Jeffrey Bean, Darrin Doyle, Matthew Roberson.

Thank you, Mom—my wide blue sky. Thank you to all my family—especially MaryClare Marlow—Soul Sister; and Dan, for your love and support; and Mike, for showing up at so many readings and showing your care. Thanks, Dad, Tom, Amy—beyond the veil. Thank you so much, Don and Gail Whitebread, for all you do.

My heart goes out to friends, writers, and editors who have been supportive over the years, including: Peter Markus, Terry Blackhawk, Matthew Olzmann, Vievee Francis, Tommye Blount, Nandi Comer, Christina Kallery, John Rybicki, Linda Nemec Foster, Mariela Griffor, Russell Thorburn, Jack Ridl, Z.G. Tomaszewski, Diane Seuss, Thomas Lynch, Keith Taylor, David James, David Sullivan, Rosie King, Sean Thomas Dougherty, Jessie Lendennie, Siobhán Hutson, Aimee Nezhukumatathil, Melissa Crowe, Scott Beal—and many others, with deep apologies for any accidental omissions. Special thanks to David Biedenbender, for finding so much music in my poems. Dennis Hinrichsen—this book wouldn't have been what it is without your close eye, your sharp blade. Thank you.

Thank you, most of all: Denise—my life's bright star. Thank you, Gabriel and Magdalena, who complete our constellation. All three of you: the hearts aglow inside my heart—forever.

ABOUT THE AUTHOR

Robert Fanning is the author of four previous full-length collections of poetry: *Severance, Our Sudden Museum, American Prophet* and *The Seed Thieves*, as well as three chapbooks: *Prince of the Air, Sheet Music,* and *Old Bright Wheel.* His poems have appeared in *Poetry, Ploughshares, Shenandoah, Gulf Coast, The Atlanta Review, Waxwing, THRUSH, Diode, The Common*, and many other journals. He is a professor of English at Central Michigan University as well as the founder and facilitator of the Wellspring Literary Series in Mt. Pleasant, Michigan.